Critical Miscellanies
Vol.- II
Essay 4: Joseph De Maistre

By

John Morley

Critical Miscellanies
Vol.- II
Essay 4: Joseph De Maistre

by John Morley

ISBN: 978-93-60463-85-4

Published by

DOUBLE 9 BOOKS

2/13-B, Ansari Road
Daryaganj, New Delhi – 110002
info@double9books.com
www.double9books.com
Tel. 011-40042856

ABOUT THE AUTHOR

JOHN MORLEY Born on December 24, 1838, John Morley was the 1st Viscount Morley of Blackburn, OM, PC, FRS, FBA. He died on September 23, 1923, and was a British Liberal politician, author, and newspaper editor. He started out as a reporter in the North of England and then became editor of the newly liberal Pall Mall Gazette from 1880 to 1883. In 1883, he was chosen as a Liberal Party Member of Parliament (MP). In 1886, 1892, and 1895, he was Chief Secretary for Ireland. From 1905 to 1910 and again in 1911, he was Secretary of State for India. From 1910 to 1914, he was Lord President of the Council. Morley was a well-known political analyst and wrote a biography of William Gladstone, who was his hero. His works and "reputation as the last of the great nineteenth-century Liberals" made Morley famous. He was against the Second Boer War and empire. He believed that Ireland should have Home Rule. He quit the government in August 1914 because he didn't want Britain to join the First World War as a Russian friend.

CONTENTS

JOSEPH DE MAISTRE

Owing to causes which lie tolerably near the surface, the remarkable Catholic reaction which took place in France at the beginning of the present century, has never received in England the attention that it deserves; not only for its striking interest as an episode in the history of European thought, but also for its peculiarly forcible and complete presentation of those ideas with which what is called the modern spirit is supposed to be engaged in deadly war. For one thing, the Protestantism of England strips a genuinely Catholic movement of speculation of that pressing and practical importance which belongs to it in countries where nearly all spiritual sentiment, that has received any impression of religion at all, unavoidably runs in Catholic forms. With us the theological reaction against the ideas of the eighteenth was not and could not be other than Protestant. The defence and reinstatement of Christianity in each case was conducted, as might have been expected, with reference to the dominant creed and system of the country. If Coleridge had been a Catholic, his works thus newly coloured by an alien creed would have been read by a small sect only, instead of exercising as they did a wide influence over the whole nation, reaching people through those usual conduits of press and pulpit, by which the products of philosophic thought are conveyed to unphilosophic minds. As naturally in France, hostility to all those influences which were believed to have brought about the Revolution, to sensationalism in metaphysics, to atheism in what should have been theology, to the notion of sovereignty of peoples in politics, inevitably sought a rallying-point in a renewed allegiance to that prodigious spiritual system which had fostered the germs of order and social feeling in Europe, and whose name remains even now in the days of its ruin, as the most permanent symbol and exemplar of stable organisation. Another reason for English indifference to this movement is the rapidity with which here, as elsewhere, dust gathers thickly round the memory of the champions of lost causes. Some of the most excellent of human characteristics—intensity of belief, for example, and a fervid anxiety to realise aspirations—unite with some of the least excellent of them, to make us too habitually forget that, as Mill has said, the best adherents of a fallen standard in philosophy, in religion, in politics, are usually next in all good qualities of understanding and sentiment to the best of those who lead the van of the force that triumphs. Men are not so anxious as they should be, considering the infinite diversity of effort that goes to the advancement of mankind, to pick up the fragments of truth and positive contribution, that so nothing be lost, and as a consequence the writings of antagonists with whom we are believed to have nothing in common, lie unexamined and disregarded.

In the case of the group of writers who, after a century of criticism, ventured once more with an intrepid confidence—differing fundamentally from the tone of preceding apologists in the Protestant camp, who were nearly as critical as the men they refuted—to vindicate not the bare outlines of Christian faith, but the entire scheme, in its extreme manifestation, of the most ancient and severely maligned of all Christian organisations, this apathy is very much to be regretted on several grounds. In the first place, it is impossible to see intelligently to the bottom of the momentous spirit of ultramontanism, which is so deep a difficulty of continental Europe, and which, touching us in Ireland, is perhaps already one of our own deepest difficulties, without comprehending in its best shape the theory on which ultramontanism rests. And this theory it is impossible to seize thoroughly, without some knowledge of the ideas of its most efficient defenders in its earlier years. Secondly, it is among these ideas that we have to look for the representation in their most direct, logical, uncompromising, and unmistakable form of those theological ways of regarding life and prescribing right conduct, whose more or less rapidly accelerated destruction is the first condition of the further elevation of humanity, as well in power of understanding as in morals and spirituality. In all contests of this kind there is the greatest and most obvious advantage in being able to see your enemy full against the light. Thirdly, in one or two respects, the Catholic reactionaries at the beginning of the century insisted very strongly on principles of society which the general thought of the century before had almost entirely dropped out of sight, and which we who, in spite of many differences, still sail down the same great current, and are propelled by the same great tide, are accustomed almost equally either to leave in the background of speculation, or else deliberately to deny and suppress. Such we may account the importance which they attach to organisation, and the value they set upon a common spiritual faith and doctrine as a social basis. That the form which the recognition of these principles is destined to assume will at all correspond to their hopes and anticipations, is one of the most unlikely things possible. This, however, need not detract from the worth for our purpose of their exposition of the principles themselves. Again, the visible traces of the impression made by the writings of this school on the influential founder of the earliest Positivist system, are sufficiently deep and important to make some knowledge of them of the highest historical interest, both to those who accept and those who detest that system.

At the beginning of the nineteenth century, there were three chief schools of thought, the Sensational, the Catholic, and the Eclectic; or as it may be put in other terms, the Materialist, the Theological, and the Spiritualist. The first looked for the sources of knowledge, the sanction of morals, the inspiring fountain and standard of æsthetics, to the outside of men, to matter, and the impressions made by matter on the corporeal senses. The second looked to divine revelation, authority and the traditions of the Church. The third, steering a middle course, looked partly within and partly without, relied partly on the senses, partly on revelation and history, but still more on a certain internal consciousness of a direct and immediate kind, which is the supreme and reconciling judge of the reports alike of the senses, of history, of divine revelation.[1] Each of these schools had many exponents. The three most conspicuous champions of revived Catholicism were De Maistre, De Bonald, and Chateaubriand. The last of them, the author of the *Génie du Christianisme*, was effective in France because he is so deeply sentimental, but he was too little trained in speculation, and too little equipped with knowledge, to be fairly taken as the best intellectual representative of their way of thinking. De Bonald was of much heavier calibre. He really thought, while Chateaubriand only felt, and the *Législation Primitive* and the *Pensées sur Divers Sujets* contain much that an enemy of the school will find it worth while to read, in spite of an artificial, and, if a foreigner may judge, a detestable style.

De Maistre was the greatest of the three, and deserves better than either of the others to stand as the type of the school for many reasons. His style is so marvellously lucid, that, notwithstanding the mystical, or, as he said, the illuminist side of his mind, we can never be in much doubt about his meaning, which is not by any means the case with Bonald. To say nothing of his immensely superior natural capacity, De Maistre's extensive reading in the literature of his foes was a source of strength, which might indeed have been thought indispensable, if only other persons had not attacked the same people as he did, without knowing much or anything at all at first-hand about them. Then he goes over the whole field of allied subjects, which we have a right to expect to have handled by anybody with a systematic view of the origin of knowledge, the meaning of ethics, the elements of social order and progressiveness, the government and scheme of the universe. And above all, his writings are penetrated with the air of reality and life, which comes of actual participation in the affairs of that world with which social philosophers have to deal. Lamennais had in many respects a finer mind than De Maistre, but the conclusions in which he was finally landed, no less than his liberal aims, prevent him from being an example of the truly Catholic reaction. He obviously represented the Revolution, or the critical spirit, within the Catholic limits, while De Maistre's ruling idea was, in his own trenchant phrase, '*absolument tuer l'esprit du dix-huitième siècle.*' On all these accounts he appears to be the fittest expositor of those conceptions which the anarchy that closed the eighteenth century provoked into systematic existence.

I.

Joseph de Maistre was born at Chambéry in the year 1754.[2] His family was the younger branch of a stock in Languedoc, which about the beginning of the seventeenth century divided itself into two, one remaining in France, the other establishing itself in Piedmont. It is not wonderful that the descendants of the latter, settled in a country of small extent and little political importance, placed a high value on their kinship with an ancient line in the powerful kingdom of France. Joseph de Maistre himself was always particularly anxious to cultivate close relations with his French kinsfolk, partly from the old aristocratic feeling of blood, and partly from his intellectual appreciation of the gifts of the French mind, and its vast influence as an universal propagating power. His father held a high office in the government of Savoy, and enjoyed so eminent a reputation that on his death both the Senate and the King of Sardinia deliberately recorded their appreciation of his loss as a public calamity. His mother is said to have been a woman of lofty and devout character, and her influence over her eldest son was exceptionally strong and tender. He used to declare in after life that he was as docile in her hands as the youngest of his sisters. Among other marks of his affectionate submission to parental authority, we are told that during the whole time of his residence at Turin, where he followed a course of law, he never read a single book without previously writing to Chambéry to one or other of his parents for their sanction. Such traditions linger in families, and when he came to have children of his own, they too read nothing of which their father had not been asked to express his approbation. De Maistre's early education was directed by the Jesuits; and as might have been expected from the generous susceptibility of his temper, he never ceased to think of them with warm esteem. To the end of his life he remembered the gloom which fell upon the household, though he was not nine years old at the time, when the news arrived of the edict of 1764, abolishing the Society in the kingdom of France. One element of his education he commemorates in a letter to his favourite daughter. 'Let your brother,' he says, 'work hard at the French poets. Let him learn them by heart, especially the incomparable Racine; never mind whether he understands him yet or not. I didn't understand him when my mother used to come repeating his verses by my bedside, and lulled me to sleep with her fine voice to the sound of that inimitable music. I knew hundreds of lines long before I knew how to read; and it is thus that my ears, accustomed betimes to this ambrosia, have never since been able to endure any sourer draught.'

After his law studies at the University of Turin, then highly renowned for its jurisconsults, the young De Maistre went through the successive stages of an official career, performing various duties in the public administration, and possessing among other honours a seat in the Senate, over which his father presided. He led a tranquil life at Chambéry, then as at all other times an ardent reader and student. Unaided he taught himself five languages. English he mastered so perfectly, that though he could not follow it when spoken, he could read a book in that tongue with as much ease as if it had been in his own. To Greek and German he did not apply himself until afterwards, and he never acquired the same proficiency in them as in English, French, Italian, Latin, and Spanish. To be ignorant of German then, it will be remembered, was not what it would be now, to be without one of the literary senses.

Like nearly every other great soldier of reaction, he showed in his early life a decided inclination for new ideas. The truth that the wildest extravagances of youthful aspiration are a better omen of a vigorous and enlightened manhood than the decorous and ignoble faith in the perfection of existing arrangements, was not belied in the case of De Maistre. His intelligence was of too hard and exact a kind to inspire him with the exalted schemes that present themselves to those more nobly imaginative minds who dream dreams and see visions. He projected no Savoyard emigration to the banks of the Susquehanna or Delaware, to found millennial societies and pantisocratic unions. These generous madnesses belong to men of more poetic temper. But still, in spite of the deadening influences of officialism and relations with a court, De Maistre had far too vigorous and active a character to subside without resistance into the unfruitful ways of obstruction and social complacency. It is one of the most certain marks, we may be sure, of a superior spirit, that the impulses earliest awakened by its first fresh contact with the facts of the outer world are those which quicken a desire for the improvement of the condition of society, the increase of the happiness of men, the amelioration of human destiny. With this unwritten condition of human nature De Maistre, like other men of his mental calibre, is found to have complied. He incurred the suspicion and ill-will of most of those by whom he was immediately surrounded, by belonging to a Reform Lodge at Chambéry. The association was one of a perfectly harmless character, but being an association, it diffused a tarnishing vapour of social disaffection and insurgency over the names of all who ventured to belong to it, and De Maistre was pointed out to the Sardinian court as a man with leanings towards new things, and therefore one of whom it were well to beware. There was little ground for apprehension. In very small countries there is seldom room enough for the growth of a spirit of social revolution; not at least until some great and dominant country has released the forces of destruction. So, when the menacing sounds of the approaching hurricane in France grew heavy in the air, the little lodge at Chambéry voluntarily dissolved itself, and De Maistre was deputed to convey to the king, Victor Amadeo iii., the honourable assurance of its members that they had assembled for the last time.

In 1786, at the age of thirty-two, De Maistre had married, and when the storm burst which destroyed all the hopes of his life, he was the father of two children. In one of his gay letters to a venerable lady who was on intimate terms with them both, he has left a picture of his wife, which is not any less interesting for what it reveals of his own character. 'The contrast between us two is the very strangest in the world. For me, as you may have found out, I am the *pococurante* senator, and above all things very free in saying what I think. She, on the contrary, will take care that it is noon before allowing that the sun has risen, for fear of committing herself. She knows what must be done or what must not be done on the tenth of October 1808, at ten o'clock in the morning, to avoid some inconvenience which otherwise would come to pass at midnight between the fifteenth and sixteenth of March 1810. "But, my dear husband, you pay attention to nothing; you believe that nobody is thinking of any harm. Now I know, I have been told, I have guessed, I foresee, I warn you," etc. "Come now, my dear, leave me alone. You are only wasting your time: I foresee that I shall never foresee things: that's your business." She is the supplement to me, and hence when I am separated from her, as I am now, I suffer absurdly from being obliged to think about my own affairs; I would rather have to chop wood all day.... My children ought to kiss her very steps; for my part, I have no gift for education. She has such a gift, that I look upon it as nothing less than the eighth endowment of the Holy Ghost; I mean a certain fond persecution by which it is given her to torment her children from morning to night to do something, not to do something, to learn—and yet without for a moment losing their tender affection for her. How can she manage it? I cannot make it out.' She was laughingly called by himself and her friends, Madame Prudence. It is certain that few women have found more necessity for the qualities implied in this creditable nickname.

They had not been married many years before they were overtaken by irreparable disaster. The French Revolution broke out, and Savoy was invaded by the troops of the new Republic. Count De Maistre, with his wife and children, fled from Chambéry across the Alps to Aosta. '*Ma chère amie,*' he said to his wife, by the side of a great rock which he never afterwards forgot, 'the step that we are taking to-day is irrevocable; it decides our lot for life;' and the presentiment was true. Soon the *Loi des Allobroges* was promulgated, which enjoined upon all who had left their homes in Savoy to return instantly, under pain of confiscation of all their property. It was the very depth of winter. Madame de Maistre was in the ninth month of her pregnancy. She knew that her husband would endure anything rather than expose her to the risks of a journey in such a season. So, urged by a desire to save something from the wreck of their fortune by compliance with the French decree, she seized the opportunity of her husband's absence at Turin, and started for Savoy without acquainting him with her design. She crossed the Great St. Bernard in the beginning of January on the back of a mule, accompanied by her two little children wrapped in blankets. The Count, on his return to Aosta two or three days afterwards, forthwith set off in her steps, in the trembling expectation of finding her dead or dying in some Alpine hovel. But the favour of fate and a stout heart brought her safe to Chambéry, where shortly afterwards she was joined by her husband. The authorities vainly tendered him the oath, vainly bade him inscribe his name on the register of citizens; and when they asked him for a contribution to support the war, he replied curtly that he did not give money to kill his brothers in the service of the King of Sardinia. As soon as his wife was delivered of their third child, whom he was destined not to see again for nearly twenty years, he quitted her side, abandoned his property and his country, and took refuge at Lausanne, where in time his wife and his two eldest children once more came to him.

Gibbon tells us how a swarm of emigrants, escaping from the public ruin, was attracted by the vicinity, the manners, and the language of Lausanne. 'They are entitled to our pity,' he reflected, 'and they may claim our esteem, but they cannot in their present state of mind and fortune contribute much to our amusement. Instead of looking down as calm and idle spectators on the theatre of Europe, our domestic harmony is somewhat embittered by the infusion of party spirit.' Gibbon died in London almost at the very moment that De Maistre arrived at Lausanne, but his account of things remained true, and political feuds continued to run as high as ever. Among the people with whom De Maistre was thrown was Madame de Staël. 'As we had not been to the same school,' he says, 'either in theology or in politics, we had some scenes enough to make one die of laughter; still without quarrelling. Her father, who was then alive, was the friend and relative of people that I love with all my heart, and that I would not vex for all the world. So I allowed the *émigrés* who surrounded us to cry out as they would, without ever drawing the sword.' De Maistre thought he never came across a head so completely turned wrong as Madame de Staël's, the infallible consequence, as he took it to be, of modern philosophy operating upon a woman's nature. He once said of her: 'Ah! if Madame de Staël had been Catholic, she would have been adorable, instead of famous.' We can believe that his position among the French *émigrés* was not particularly congenial. For though they hated the Revolution, they had all drunk of the waters of the eighteenth century philosophy, and De Maistre hated this philosophy worse than he hated the Revolution itself. Then again, they would naturally vapour about the necessities of strong government. 'Yes,' said the Savoyard exile, 'but be quite sure that, to make the monarchy strong, you must rest it on the laws, avoiding everything arbitrary, too frequent commissions, and all ministerial jobberies.' We may well believe how unsavoury this rational and just talk was to people who meant by strong government a system that should restore to them their old prerogatives of anti-social oppression and selfish corruption. The order that De Maistre vindicated was a very different thing from the deadly and poisonous order which was the object of the prayers of the incorrigible royalists around him.

After staying three years at Lausanne, De Maistre went to Turin, but shortly afterwards the Sardinian king, at the end of a long struggle, was forced to succumb to the power of the French, then in the full tide of success. Bonaparte's brilliant Italian campaign needs no words here. The French entered Turin, and De Maistre, being an *émigré*, had to leave it. Furnished with a false passport, and undergoing a thousand hardships and dangers, he made his way, once more in the depth of a severe winter (1797), to Venice. He went part of the way down the Po in a small trading ship, crowded with ladies, priests, monks, soldiers, and a bishop. There was only one small fire on board, at which all the cooking had to be done, and where the unhappy passengers had to keep themselves warm as they could. At night they were confined each to a space about three planks broad, separated from neighbours by pieces of canvas hanging from a rope above. Each bank of the river was lined by military posts—the left by the Austrians, and the right by the French; and the danger of being fired into was constantly present to aggravate the misery of overcrowding, scanty food, and bitter cold. Even this wretchedness was surpassed by the hardships which confronted the exiles at Venice. The physical distress endured here by De Maistre and his unfortunate family exceeded that of any other period of their wanderings. He was cut off from the court, and from all his relations and friends, and reduced for the means of existence to a few fragments of silver plate, which had somehow been saved from the universal wreck. This slender resource grew less day by day, and when that was exhausted the prospect was a blank. The student of De Maistre's philosophy may see in what crushing personal anguish some of its most sinister growths had their roots. When the cares of beggary come suddenly upon a man in middle life, they burn very deep. Alone, and starving for a cause that is dear to him, he might encounter the grimness of fate with a fortitude in which there should be many elevating and consoling elements. But the destiny is intolerably hard which condemns a man of humane mould, as De Maistre certainly was, to look helplessly on the physical pains of a tender woman and famishing little ones. The anxieties that press upon his heart in such calamity as this are too sharp, too tightened, and too sordid for him to draw a single free breath, or to raise his eyes for a single moment of relief from the monstrous perplexity that chokes him. The hour of bereavement has its bitterness, but the bitterness is gradually suffused with soft reminiscence. The grip of beggary leaves a mark on such a character as De Maistre's which no prosperity of after days effaces. The seeming inhumanity of his theory of life, which is so revolting to comfortable people like M. Villemain, was in truth the only explanation of his own cruel sufferings in which he could find any solace. It was not that he hated mankind, but that his destiny looked as if God hated him, and this was a horrible moral complexity out of which he could only extricate himself by a theory in which pain and torment seem to stand out as the main facts in human existence.

To him, indeed, prosperity never came. Hope smiled on him momentarily, but, in his own words: 'It was only a flash in the night.' While he was in Venice, the armies of Austria and Russia reconquered the north of Italy, and Charles Emanuel iv., in the natural anticipation that the allies would at once restore his dominions, hastened forward. Austria, however, as De Maistre had seen long before, was indifferent or even absolutely hostile to Sardinian interests, and she successfully opposed Charles Emanuel's restoration. The king received the news of the perfidy of his nominal ally at Florence, but not until after he had made arrangements for rewarding the fidelity of some of his most loyal adherents.

It was from Florence that De Maistre received the king's nomination to the chief place in the government of the island of Sardinia. Through the short time of his administration here, he was overwhelmed with vexations only a little more endurable than the physical distresses which had weighed him down at Venice. During the war, justice had been administered in a grossly irregular manner. Hence, people had taken the law into their own hands, and retaliation had completed the round of wrong-doing. The taxes were collected with great difficulty. The higher class exhibited an invincible repugnance to paying their debts. Some of these difficulties in the way of firm and orderly government were insuperable, and De Maistre vexed his soul in an unequal and only partially successful contest. In after years, amid the miseries of his life in Russia, he wrote to his brother thus: 'Sometimes in moments of solitude that I multiply as much as I possibly can, I throw my head back on the cushion of my sofa, and there with my four walls around me, far from all that is dear to me, confronted by a sombre and impenetrable future, I recall the days when in a little town that you know well'—he meant Cagliari—'with my head resting on another sofa, and only seeing around our own exclusive circle (good heavens, what an impertinence!) little men and little things, I used to ask myself: "Am I then condemned to live and die in this place, like a limpet on a rock?" I suffered bitterly; my head was overloaded, wearied, flattened, by the enormous weight of Nothing.'

But presently a worse thing befell him. In 1802 he received an order from the king to proceed to St. Petersburg as envoy extraordinary and minister plenipotentiary at the court of Russia. Even from this bitter proof of devotion to his sovereign he did not shrink. He had to tear himself from his wife and children, without any certainty when so cruel a separation would be likely to end; to take up new functions which the circumstances of the time rendered excessively difficult; while the petty importance of the power he represented, and its mendicant attitude in Europe, robbed his position of that public distinction and dignity which may richly console a man for the severest private sacrifice. It is a kind destiny which veils their future from mortal men. Fifteen years passed before De Maistre's exile came to a close. From 1802 to 1817 he did not quit the inhospitable latitudes of northern Russia.

De Maistre's letters during this desolate period furnish a striking picture of his manner of life and his mental state. We see in them his most prominent characteristics strongly marked. Not even the painfulness of the writer's situation ever clouds his intrepid and vigorous spirit. Lively and gallant sallies of humour to his female friends, sagacious judgments on the position of Europe to political people, bits of learned criticism for erudite people, tender and playful chat with his two daughters, all these alternate with one another with the most delightful effect. Whether he is writing to his little girl whom he has never known, or to the king of Sardinia, or to some author who sends him a book, or to a minister who has found fault with his diplomacy, there is in all alike the same constant and remarkable play of a bright and penetrating intellectual light, coloured by a humour that is now and then a little sardonic, but more often is genial and lambent. There is a certain semi-latent quality of hardness lying at the bottom of De Maistre's style, both in his letters and in his more elaborate compositions. His writings seem to recall the flavour and bouquet of some of the fortifying and stimulating wines of Burgundy, from which time and warmth have not yet drawn out a certain native roughness that lingers on the palate.

This hardness, if one must give the quality a name that only imperfectly describes it, sprang not from any original want of impressionableness or sensibility of nature, but partly from the relentless buffetings which he had to endure at the hands of fortune, and partly from the preponderance which had been given to the rational side of his mind by long habits of sedulous and accurate study. Few men knew so perfectly as he knew how to be touching without ceasing to be masculine, nor how to go down into the dark pits of human life without forgetting the broad sunlight, nor how to keep habitually close to visible and palpable fact while eagerly addicted to speculation. His contemplations were perhaps somewhat too near the ground; they led him into none of those sublimer regions of subtle feeling where the rarest human spirits have loved to travel; we do not think of his mind among those who have gone

Voyaging through strange seas of thought alone.

If this kind of temper, strong, keen, frank, and a little hard and mordent, brought him too near a mischievous disbelief in the dignity of men and their lives, at least it kept him well away from morbid weakness in ethics, and from beating the winds in metaphysics. But of this we shall see more in considering his public pieces than can be gathered from his letters.

The discomforts of De Maistre's life at St. Petersburg were extreme. The dignity of his official style and title was an aggravation of the exceeding straitness of his means. The ruined master could do little to mitigate the ruin of his servant. He had to keep up the appearance of an ambassador on the salary of a clerk. 'This is the second winter,' he writes to his brother in 1810, 'that I have gone through without a pelisse, which is exactly like going without a shirt at Cagliari. When I come from court a very sorry lackey throws a common cloak over my shoulders.' The climate suited him better than he had expected; and in one letter he vows that he was the only living being in Russia who had passed two winters without fur boots and a fur hat. It was considered indispensable that he should keep a couple of servants; so, for his second, De Maistre was obliged to put up with a thief, whom he rescued under the shelter of ambassadorial privilege from the hands of justice, on condition that he would turn honest. The Austrian ambassador, with whom he was on good terms, would often call to take him out to some entertainment. 'His fine servants mount my staircase groping their way in the dark, and we descend preceded by a servant carrying *luminare minus quam ut præesset nocti.*' 'I am certain,' he adds pleasantly, 'that they make songs about me in their Austrian patois. Poor souls! it is well they can amuse themselves.'

Sometimes he was reduced so far as to share the soup of his valet, for lack of richer and more independent fare. Then he was constantly fretted by enemies at home, who disliked his trenchant diplomacy, and distrusted the strength and independence of a mind which was too vigorous to please the old-fashioned ministers of the Sardinian court. These chagrins he took as a wise man should. They disturbed him less than his separation from his family. 'Six hundred leagues away from you all,' he writes to his brother, 'the thoughts of my family, the reminiscences of childhood, transport me with sadness.' Visions of his mother's saintly face haunted his chamber; almost gloomier still was the recollection of old intimates with whom he had played, lived, argued, and worked for years, and yet who now no longer bore him in mind. There are not many glimpses of this melancholy in the letters meant for the eye of his beloved *trinité féminine*, as he playfully called his wife and two daughters. '*A quoi bon vous attrister*,' he asked bravely, '*sans raison et sans profit?*' Occasionally he cannot help letting out to them how far his mind is removed from composure. 'Every day as I return home I found my house as desolate as if it was yesterday you left me. In society the same fancy pursues me, and scarcely ever quits me.' Music, as might be surmised in so sensitive a nature, drove him almost beside himself with its mysterious power of intensifying the dominant emotion. 'Whenever by any chance I hear the harpsichord,' he says, 'melancholy seizes me. The sound of the violin gives me such a heavy heart, that I am fain to leave the company and hasten home.' He tossed in his bed at night, thinking he heard the sound of weeping at Turin, making a thousand efforts to picture to himself the looks of that 'orphan child of a living father' whom he had never known, wondering if ever he should know her, and battling with a myriad of black phantoms that seemed to rustle in his curtains. 'But you, M. de Chevalier,' he said apologetically to the correspondent to whom he told these dismal things, 'you are a father, you know the cruel dreams of a waking man; if you were not of the profession I would not allow my pen to write you this jeremiad.' As De Maistre was accustomed to think himself happy if he got three hours' sound sleep in the night, these sombre and terrible vigils were ample enough to excuse him if he had allowed them to overshadow all other things. But the vigour of his intellect was too strenuous, and his curiosity and interest in every object of knowledge too inextinguishable. 'After all,' he said, 'the only thing to do is to put on a good face, and to march to the place of torture with a few friends to console you on the way. This is the charming image under which I picture my present situation. Mark you,' he added, 'I always count books among one's consoling friends.'

In one of the most gay and charming of his letters, apologising to a lady for the remissness of his correspondence, he explains that diplomacy and books occupy every moment. 'You will admit, madam, there is no possibility of one's shutting up books entirely. Nay, more than ever, I feel myself burning with the feverish thirst for knowledge. I have had an access of it which I cannot describe to you. The most curious books literally run after me, and hurry voluntarily to place themselves in my hands. As soon as diplomacy gives me a moment of breathing-time I rush headlong to that favourite pasture, to that ambrosia of which the mind can never have enough—

Et voilà ce qui fait que votre ami est muet.'

He thinks himself happy if, by refusing invitations to dinner, he can pass a whole day without stirring from his house. 'I read, I write, I study; for after all one must know something.' In his hours of depression he fancied that he only read and worked, not for the sake of the knowledge, but to stupefy and tire himself out, if that were possible.

As a student De Maistre was indefatigable. He never belonged to that languid band who hoped to learn difficult things by easy methods. The only way, he warned his son, is to shut your door, to say that you are not within, and to work. 'Since they have set themselves to teach us how we ought to learn the dead languages, you can find nobody who knows them; and it is amusing enough that people who don't know them, should be so obstinately bent on demonstrating the vices of the methods employed by us who do know them.' He was one of those wise and laborious students who do not read without a pen in their hands. He never shrank from the useful toil of transcribing abundantly from all the books he read everything that could by any possibility eventually be of service to him in his inquiries. His notebooks were enormous. As soon as one of them was filled, he carefully made up an index of its contents, numbered it, and placed it on a shelf with its unforgotten predecessors. In one place he accidentally mentions that he had some thirty of these folios over the head of his writing-table.

'If I am a pedant at home,' he said, 'at least I am as little as possible a pedant out of doors.' In the evening he would occasionally seek the society of ladies, by way of recovering some of that native gaiety of heart which had hitherto kept him alive. 'I blow on this spark,' to use his own words, 'just as an old woman blows among the ashes to get a light for her lamp.' A student and a thinker, De Maistre was also a man of the world, and he may be added to the long list of writers who have shown that to take an active part in public affairs and mix in society give a peculiar life, reality, and force to both scholarship and speculation. It was computed at that time that the author of a philosophic piece could not safely count upon more than a hundred and fifty readers in Russia; and hence, we might be sure, even if we had not De Maistre's word for it, that away from his own house he left his philosophy behind. The vehemence of his own convictions did not prevent him from being socially tolerant to others who hated them. 'If I had the good fortune to be among his acquaintances,' he wrote of a heretical assailant, 'he would see that among the people with convictions it would be hard to find one so free from prejudice as I am. I have many friends among the Protestants, and now that their system is tottering, they are all the dearer to me.' In spite of his scanty means, his shabby valet, his threadbare cloak, and the humbleness of his diplomatic position, the fire and honesty of his character combined with his known ability to place him high in the esteem of the society of St. Petersburg. His fidelity, devotion, and fortitude, mellowed by many years and by meditative habits, and tinged perhaps by the patrician consciousness of birth, formed in him a modest dignity of manner which men respected. They perceived it to be no artificial assumption, but the outward image of a lofty and self-respecting spirit. His brother diplomatists, even the representatives of France, appear to have treated him with marked consideration. His letters prove him to have been a favourite among ladies. The Emperor Alexander showed him considerable kindness of the cheap royal sort. He conferred on his brother, Xavier de Maistre, a post in one of the public museums, while to the Sardinian envoy's son he gave a commission in the Russian service.

The first departure of this son for the campaign of 1807 occasioned some of the most charming passages in De Maistre's letters, both to the young soldier himself and to others. For though without a touch of morbid expansiveness, he never denied himself the solace of opening his heart to a trusted friend, and a just reserve with strangers did not hinder a humane and manly confidence with intimates. 'This morning,' he wrote to his stripling, soon after he had joined the army, 'I felt a tightening at my heart when a pet dog came running in and jumped upon your bed, where he finds you no more. He soon perceived his mistake, and said clearly enough, after his own fashion: *I am mistaken; where can he be then?* As for me I have felt all that you will feel, if ever you pursue this mighty trade of being a father.' And then he begs of his son if he should find himself with a tape line in his hand, that he will take his exact measure and forward it. Soon came the news of the battle of Friedland, and the unhappy father thought he read the fate of his son in the face of every acquaintance he met. And so it was in later campaigns, as De Maistre records in correspondence that glows with tender and healthy solicitude. All this is worth dwelling upon, for two reasons. First, because De Maistre has been too much regarded and spoken of as a man of cold sensibility, and little moved by the hardships which fill the destiny of our unfortunate race. And, secondly, because his own keen acquaintance with mental anguish helps us to understand the zeal with which he attempts to reconcile the blind cruelty and pain and torture endured by mortals with the benignity and wisdom of the immortal. 'After all,' he used to say, 'there are only two real evils—remorse and disease.' This is true enough for an apophthegm, but as a matter of fact it never for an instant dulled his sensibility to far less supreme forms of agony than the recollection of irreparable pain struck into the lives of others. It is interesting and suggestive to recall how a later publicist viewed the ills that dwarf our little lives. 'If I were asked to class human miseries,' said Tocqueville, 'I would do so in this order: first, Disease; second, Death; third, Doubt.' At a later date, he altered the order, and deliberately declared doubt to be the most insupportable of all evils, worse than death itself. But Tocqueville was an aristocrat, as Guizot once told him, who accepted his defeat. He stood on the brink of the great torrent of democracy, and shivered. De Maistre was an aristocrat too, but he was incapable of knowing what doubt or hesitation meant. He never dreamt that his cause was lost, and he mocked and defied the Revolution to the end. We easily see how natures of this sort, ardent, impetuous, unflinching, find themselves in the triumphant paths that lead to remorse at their close, and how they thus come to feel remorse rather than doubt as the consummate agony of the human mind.

Having had this glimpse of De Maistre's character away from his books, we need not linger long over the remaining events of his life. In 1814 his wife and two daughters joined him in the Russian capital. Two years later an outburst of religious fanaticism caused the sudden expulsion of the Jesuits from Russia, to De Maistre's deep mortification. Several conversions had taken place from the Orthodox to the Western faith, and these inflamed the Orthodox party, headed by the Prince de Galitzin, the minister of public worship, with violent theological fury. De Maistre, whose intense attachment to his own creed was well known, fell under suspicion of having connived at these conversions, and the Emperor himself went so far as to question him. 'I told him,' De Maistre says, 'that I had never changed the faith of any of his subjects, but that if any of them had by chance made me a sharer of their confidence, neither honour nor conscience would have allowed me to tell them that they were wrong.' This kind of dialogue between a sovereign and an ambassador implied a situation plainly unfavourable to effective diplomacy. The envoy obtained his recall, and after twenty-five years' absence returned to his native country (1817). On his way home, it may be noticed, De Maistre passed a few days in Paris, and thus, for the first and last time, one of the most eminent of modern French writers found himself on French soil.

The king accorded De Maistre an honourable reception, conferred upon him a high office and a small sum of money, and lent his ear to other counsellors. The philosopher, though insisting on declaring his political opinions, then, as ever, unwaveringly anti-revolutionary, threw himself mainly upon that literary composition which had been his solace in yet more evil days than these. It was at this time that he gave to the world the supreme fruit of nearly half a century of study, meditation, and contact with the world, in *Du Pape, Les Soirées de Saint Pétersbourg*, and *L'Eglise Gallicane*. Their author did not live long to enjoy the vast discussion which they occasioned, nor the reputation that they have since conferred upon his name. He died in February 1821 after such a life as we have seen.

II.

It is not at all surprising that they upon whom the revolutionary deluge came should have looked with indiscriminating horror and affright on all the influences which in their view had united first to gather up, and then to release the destructive flood. The eighteenth century to men like De Maistre seemed an infamous parenthesis, mysteriously interposed between the glorious age of Bossuet and Fénelon, and that yet brighter era for faith and the Church which was still to come in the good time of Divine Providence. The philosophy of the last century, he says on more than one occasion, will form one of the most shameful epochs of the human mind: it never praised even good men except for what was bad in them. He looked upon the gods whom that century had worshipped as the direct authors of the bloodshed and ruin in which their epoch had closed. The memory of mild and humane philosophers was covered with the kind of black execration that prophets of old had hurled at Baal or Moloch; Locke and Hume, Voltaire and Rousseau, were habitually spoken of as very scourges of God. From this temper two consequences naturally flowed. In the first place, while it lasted there was no hope of an honest philosophic discussion of the great questions which divide speculative minds. Moderation and impartiality were virtues of almost superhuman difficulty for controversialists who had made up their minds that it was their opponents who had erected the guillotine, confiscated the sacred property of the church, slaughtered and banished her children, and filled the land with terror and confusion. It is hard amid the smoking ruins of the homestead to do full justice to the theoretical arguments of the supposed authors of the conflagration. Hence De Maistre, though, as has been already said, intimately acquainted with the works of his foes in the letter, was prevented by the vehemence of his antipathy to the effects which he attributed to them, from having any just critical estimate of their value and true spirit. 'I do not know one of these men,' he says of the philosophers of the eighteenth century, 'to whom the sacred title of honest man is quite suitable.' They are all wanting in probity. Their very names '*me déchirent la bouche.*' To admire Voltaire is the sign of a corrupt soul; and if anybody is drawn to the works of Voltaire, then be sure that God does not love such an one. The divine anathema is written on the very face of this arch-blasphemer; on his shameless brow, in the two extinct craters still sparkling with sensuality and hate, in that frightful *rictus* running from ear to ear, in those lips tightened by cruel malice, like a spring ready to fly back and launch forth blasphemy and sarcasm; he plunges into the mud, rolls in it, drinks of it; he surrenders his imagination to the enthusiasm of hell, which lends him all its forces; Paris crowned him, Sodom would have banished him.[3] Locke, again, did not understand himself. His distinguishing characteristics are feebleness and precipitancy of judgment. Vagueness and irresolution reign in his expressions as they do in his thoughts. He constantly exhibits that most decisive sign of mediocrity—he passes close by the greatest questions without perceiving them. In the study of philosophy, contempt for Locke is the beginning of knowledge.[4] Condillac was even more vigilantly than anybody else on his guard against his own conscience. But Hume was perhaps the most dangerous and the most guilty of all those mournful writers who will for ever accuse the last century before posterity—the one who employed the most talent with the most coolness to do most harm.[5] To Bacon De Maistre paid the compliment of composing a long refutation of his main ideas, in which Bacon's blindness, presumption, profanity, and scientific charlatanry are denounced in vehement and almost coarse terms, and treated as the natural outcome of a low morality.

It has long been the inglorious speciality of the theological school to insist in this way upon moral depravity as an antecedent condition of intellectual error. De Maistre in this respect was not unworthy of his fellows. He believed that his opponents were even worse citizens than they were bad philosophers, and it was his horror of them in the former capacity that made him so bitter and resentful against them in the latter. He could think of no more fitting image for opinions that he did not happen to believe than counterfeit money, 'which is struck in the first instance by great criminals, and is afterwards passed on by honest folk who perpetuate the crime without knowing what they do.' A philosopher of the highest class, we may be sure, does not permit himself to be drawn down from the true object of his meditations by these sinister emotions. But De Maistre belonged emphatically to minds of the second order, whose eagerness to find truth is never intense and pure enough to raise them above perturbing antipathies to persons. His whole attitude was fatal to his claim to be heard as a truth-seeker in any right sense of the term. He was not only persuaded of the general justice and inexpugnableness of the orthodox system, but he refused to believe that it was capable of being improved or supplemented by anything which a temperate and fair examination of other doctrines might peradventure be found to yield. With De Maistre there was no peradventure. Again, no speculative mind of the highest order ever mistakes, or ever moves systematically apart from, the main current of the social movement of its time. It is implied in the very definition of a thinker of supreme quality that he should detect, and be in a certain accord with, the most forward and central of the ruling tendencies of his epoch. Three-quarters of a century have elapsed since De Maistre was driven to attempt to explain the world to himself, and this interval has sufficed to show that the central conditions at that time for the permanent reorganisation of the society which had just been so violently rent in pieces, were assuredly not theological, military, nor ultramontane, but the very opposite of all these.

There was a second consequence of the conditions of the time. The catastrophe of Europe affected the matter as well as the manner of contemporary speculation. The French Revolution has become to us no more than a term, though the strangest term in a historic series. To some of the best of those who were confronted on every side by its tumult and agitation, it was the prevailing of the gates of hell, the moral disruption of the universe, the absolute and total surrender of the world to them that plough iniquity and sow wickedness. Even under ordinary circumstances few men have gone through life without encountering some triumphant iniquity, some gross and prolonged cruelty, which makes them wonder how God should allow such things to be. If we remember the aspect which the Revolution wore in the eyes of those who seeing it yet did not understand, we can imagine what dimensions this eternal enigma must have assumed in their sight. It was inevitable that the first problem to press on men with resistless urgency should be the ancient question of the method of the Creator's temporal government. What is the law of the distribution of good and evil fortune? How can we vindicate with regard to the conditions of this life, the different destinies that fall to men? How can we defend the moral ordering of a world in which the wicked and godless constantly triumph, while the virtuous and upright who retain their integrity are as frequently buffeted and put to shame?

This tremendous question has never been presented with such sublimity of expression, such noble simplicity and force of thought, as in the majestic and touching legend of Job. But its completeness, as a presentation of the human tragedy, is impaired by the excessive prosperity which is finally supposed to reward the patient hero for his fortitude. Job received twice as much as he had before, and his latter end was blessed more than his beginning. In the chronicles of actual history men fare not so. There is a terribly logical finish about some of the dealings of fate, and in life the working of a curse is seldom stayed by any dramatic necessity for a smooth consummation. Destiny is no artist. The facts that confront us are relentless. No statement of the case is adequate which maintains, by ever so delicate an implication, that in the long run and somehow it is well in temporal things with the just, and ill with the unjust. Until we have firmly looked in the face the grim truth that temporal rewards and punishments do not follow the possession or the want of spiritual or moral virtue, so long we are still ignorant what that enigma is, which speculative men, from the author of the book of Job downwards, have striven to resolve. We can readily imagine the fulness with which the question would grow up in the mind of a royalist and Catholic exile at the end of the eighteenth century.

Nothing can be more clearly put than De Maistre's answers to the question which the circumstances of the time placed before him to solve. What is the law of the distribution of good and evil fortune in this life? Is it a moral law? Do prosperity and adversity fall respectively to the just and the unjust, either individually or collectively? Has the ancient covenant been faithfully kept, that whoso hearkens diligently to the divine voice, and observes all the commandments to do them, shall be blessed in his basket and his store and in all the work of his hand? Or is God a God that hideth himself?

De Maistre perceived that the optimistic conception of the deity as benign, merciful, infinitely forgiving, was very far indeed from covering the facts. So he insisted on seeing in human destiny the ever-present hand of a stern and terrible judge, administering a Draconian code with blind and pitiless severity. God created men under conditions which left them free to choose between good and evil. All the physical evil that exists in the world is a penalty for the moral evil that has resulted from the abuse by men of this freedom of choice. For these physical calamities God is only responsible in the way in which a criminal judge is responsible for a hanging. Men cannot blame the judge for the gallows; the fault is their own in committing those offences for which hanging is prescribed beforehand as the penalty. These curses which dominate human life are not the result of the cruelty of the divine ruler, but of the folly and wickedness of mankind, who, seeing the better course, yet deliberately choose the worse. The order of the world is overthrown by the iniquities of men; it is we who have provoked the exercise of the divine justice, and called down the tokens of his vengeance. The misery and disaster that surround us like a cloak are the penalty of our crimes and the price of our expiation. As the divine St. Thomas has said: *Deus est auctor mali quod est pœna, non autem mali quod est culpa.* There is a certain quantity of wrong done over the face of the world; therefore the great Judge exacts a proportionate quantity of punishment. The total amount of evil suffered makes nice equation with the total amount of evil done; the extent of human suffering tallies precisely with the extent of human guilt. Of course you must take original sin into account, 'which explains all, and without which you can explain nothing.' 'In virtue of this primitive degradation we are subject to all sorts of physical sufferings *in general;* just as in virtue of this same degradation we are subject to all sorts of vices *in general.* This original malady therefore [which is the correlative of original sin] has no other name. It is only the capacity of suffering all evils, as original sin is only the capacity of committing all crimes.'[6] Hence all calamity is either the punishment of sins actually committed by the sufferers, or else it is the general penalty exacted for general sinfulness. Sometimes an innocent being is stricken, and a guilty being appears to escape. But is it not the same in the transactions of earthly tribunals? And yet we do not say that they are conducted without regard to justice and righteousness. 'When God punishes any society for the crimes that it has committed, he does justice as we do justice ourselves in these sorts of circumstance. A city revolts; it massacres the representatives of the sovereign; it shuts its gates against him; it defends itself against his arms; it is taken. The prince has it dismantled and deprived of all its privileges; nobody will find fault with this decision on the ground that there are innocent persons shut up in the city.'[7]

De Maistre's deity is thus a colossal Septembriseur, enthroned high in the peaceful heavens, demanding ever-renewed holocausts in the name of the public safety.

It is true, as a general rule of the human mind, that the objects which men have worshipped have improved in morality and wisdom as men themselves have improved. The quiet gods, without effort of their own, have grown holier and purer by the agitations and toil which civilise their worshippers. In other words, the same influences which elevate and widen our sense of human duty give corresponding height and nobleness to our ideas of the divine character. The history of the civilisation of the earth is the history of the civilisation of Olympus also. It will be seen that the deity whom De Maistre sets up is below the moral level of the time in respect of Punishment. In intellectual matters he vehemently proclaimed the superiority of the tenth or the twelfth over the eighteenth century, but it is surely carrying admiration for those loyal times indecently far, to seek in the vindictive sackings of revolted towns, and the miscellaneous butcheries of men, women, and babes, which then marked the vengeance of outraged sovereignty, the most apt parallel and analogy for the systematic administration of human society by its Creator. Such punishment can no longer be regarded as moral in any deep or permanent sense; it implies a gross, harsh, and revengeful character in the executioner, that is eminently perplexing and incredible to those who expect to find an idea of justice in the government of the world, at least not materially below what is attained in the clumsy efforts of uninspired publicists.

In mere point of administration, the criminal code which De Maistre put into the hands of the Supreme Being works in a more arbitrary and capricious manner than any device of an Italian Bourbon. As Voltaire asks—

> *Lisbonne, qui n'est plus, eut-elle plus de vices*
> *Que Londres, que Paris, plongés dans les délices?*
> *Lisbonne est abîmée, et l'on danse à Paris.*

Stay, De Maistre replies, look at Paris thirty years later, not dancing, but red with blood. This kind of thing is often said, even now; but it is really time to abandon the prostitution of the name of Justice to a process which brings Lewis xvi. to the block, and consigns De Maistre to poverty and exile, because Lewis xiv., the Regent, and Lewis xv. had been profligate men or injudicious rulers. The reader may remember how the unhappy Emperor Maurice as his five innocent sons were in turn murdered before his eyes, at each stroke piously ejaculated: 'Thou art just, O Lord! and thy judgments are righteous.'[8] Any name would befit this kind of transaction better than that which, in the dealings of men with one another at least, we reserve for the honourable anxiety that he should reap who has sown, that the reward should be to him who has toiled for it, and the pain to him who has deliberately incurred it. What is gained by attributing to the divine government a method tainted with every quality that could vitiate the enactment of penalties by a temporal sovereign?

We need not labour this part of the discussion further. Though conducted with much brilliance and vigour by De Maistre, it is not his most important nor remarkable contribution to thought. Before passing on to that, it is worth while to make one remark. It will be inferred from De Maistre's general position that he was no friend to physical science. Just as moderns see in the advance of the methods and boundaries of physical knowledge the most direct and sure means of displacing the unfruitful subjective methods of old, and so of renovating the entire field of human thought and activity, so did De Maistre see, as his school has seen since, that here was the stronghold of his foes. 'Ah, how dearly,' he exclaimed, 'has man paid for the natural sciences!' Not but that Providence designed that man should know something about them; only it must be in due order. The ancients were not permitted to attain to much or even any sound knowledge of physics, indisputably above us as they were in force of mind, a fact shown by the superiority of their languages which ought to silence for ever the voice of our modern pride. Why did the ancients remain so ignorant of natural science? Because they were not Christian. 'When all Europe was Christian, when the priests were the universal teachers, when all the establishments of Europe were Christianised, when theology had taken its place at the head of all instruction, and the other faculties were ranged around her like maids of honour round their queen, the human race being thus prepared, then the natural sciences were given to it.' Science must be kept in its place, for it resembles fire which, when confined in the grates prepared for it, is the most useful and powerful of man's servants; scattered about anyhow, it is the most terrible of scourges. Whence the marked supremacy of the seventeenth century, especially in France? From the happy accord of religion, science, and chivalry, and from the supremacy conceded to the first. The more perfect theology is in a country the more fruitful it is in true science; and that is why Christian nations have surpassed all others in the sciences, and that is why the Indians and Chinese will never reach us, so long as we remain respectively as we are. The more theology is cultivated, honoured, and supreme, then, other things being equal, the more perfect will human science be: that is to say, it will have the greater force and expansion, and will be the more free from every mischievous and perilous connection.[9]

Little would be gained here by serious criticism of a view of this kind from a positive point. How little, the reader will understand from De Maistre's own explanations of his principles of Proof and Evidence. 'They have called to witness against Moses,' he says, 'history, chronology, astronomy, geology, etc. The objections have disappeared before true science; but those were profoundly wise who despised them before any inquiry, or who only examined them in order to discover a refutation, but without ever doubting that there was one. Even a mathematical objection ought to be despised, for though it may be a demonstrated truth, still you will never be able to demonstrate that it contradicts a truth that has been demonstrated before.' His final formula he boldly announced in these words: '*Que toutes les fois qu'une proposition sera prouvée par le genre de preuve qui lui appartient, l'objection quelconque,* même insoluble, *ne doit plus être écoutée.*' Suppose, for example, that by a consensus of testimony it were perfectly proved that Archimedes set fire to the fleet of Marcellus by a burning-glass; then all the objections of geometry disappear. Prove if you can, and if you choose, that by certain laws a glass, in order to be capable of setting fire to the Roman fleet, must have been as big as the whole city of Syracuse, and ask me what answer I have to make to that. '*J'ai à vous répondre qu'Archimède brûla la flotte romaine avec un miroir ardent.*'

The interesting thing about such opinions as these is not the exact height and depth of their falseness, but the considerations which could recommend them to a man of so much knowledge, both of books and of the outer facts of life, and of so much natural acuteness as De Maistre. Persons who have accustomed themselves to ascertained methods of proof, are apt to look on a man who vows that if a thing has been declared true by some authority whom he respects, then that constitutes proof to him, as either the victim of a preposterous and barely credible infatuation, or else as a flat impostor. Yet De Maistre was no ignorant monk. He had no selfish or official interest in taking away the keys of knowledge, entering not in himself, and them that would enter in hindering. The true reasons for his detestation of the eighteenth-century philosophers, science, and literature, are simple enough. Like every wise man, he felt that the end of all philosophy and science is emphatically social, the construction and maintenance and improvement of a fabric under which the communities of men may find shelter, and may secure all the conditions for living their lives with dignity and service. Then he held that no truth can be harmful to society. If he found any system of opinions, any given attitude of the mind, injurious to tranquillity and the public order, he instantly concluded that, however plausible they might seem when tested by logic and demonstration, they were fundamentally untrue and deceptive. What is logic compared with eternal salvation in the next world, and the practice of virtue in this? The recommendation of such a mind as De Maistre's is the intensity of its appreciation of order and social happiness. The obvious weakness of such a mind, and the curse inherent in its influence, is that it overlooks the prime condition of all; that social order can never be established on a durable basis so long as the discoveries of scientific truth in all its departments are suppressed, or incorrectly appreciated, or socially misapplied. De Maistre did not perceive that the cause which he supported was no longer the cause of peace and tranquillity and right living, but was in a state of absolute and final decomposition, and therefore was the cause of disorder and blind wrong living. Of this we shall now see more.

III.

When the waters of the deluge of '89 began to assuage, the best minds soon satisfied themselves that the event which Bonaparte's restoration of order enabled them to look back upon with a certain tranquillity and a certain completeness, had been neither more nor less than a new irruption of barbarians into the European world. The monarchy, the nobles, and the Church, with all the ideas that gave each of them life and power, had fallen before atheists and Jacobins, as the ancient empire of Rome had fallen before Huns and Goths, Vandals and Lombards. The leaders of the revolution had succeeded one another, as Attila had come after Alaric, and as Genseric had been followed by Odoacer. The problem which presented itself was not new in the history of western civilisation; the same dissolution of old bonds which perplexed the foremost men at the beginning of the nineteenth century, had distracted their predecessors from the fifth to the eighth, though their conditions and circumstances were widely different. The practical question in both cases was just the same—how to establish a stable social order which, resting on principles that should command the assent of all, might secure the co-operation of all for its harmonious and efficient maintenance, and might offer a firm basis for the highest and best life that the moral and intellectual state of the time allowed. There were two courses open, or which seemed to be open, in this gigantic enterprise of reconstructing a society. One of them was to treat the case of the eighteenth century as if it were not merely similar to, but exactly identical with, the case of the fifth, and as if exactly the same forces which had knit Western Europe together into a compact civilisation a thousand years before, would again suffice for a second consolidation. Christianity, rising with the zeal and strength of youth out of the ruins of the Empire, and feudalism by the need of self-preservation imposing a form upon the unshapen associations of the barbarians, had between them compacted the foundations and reared the fabric of mediæval life. Why, many men asked themselves, should not Christian and feudal ideas repeat their great achievement, and be the means of reorganising the system which a blind rebellion against them had thrown into deplorable and fatal confusion? Let the century which had come to such an end be regarded as a mysteriously intercalated episode, and no more, in the long drama of faith and sovereign order. Let it pass as a sombre and pestilent stream, whose fountains no man should discover, whose waters had for a season mingled with the mightier current of the divinely allotted destiny of the race, and had then gathered themselves apart and flowed off, to end as they had begun, in the stagnation and barrenness of the desert. Philosophers and men of letters, astronomers and chemists, atheists and republicans, had shown that they were only powerful to destroy, as the Goths and the Vandals had been. They had shown that they were impotent, as the Goths and the Vandals had been, in building up again. Let men turn their faces, then, once more to that system by which in the ancient times Europe had been delivered from a relapse into eternal night.

The second course was very different from this. The minds to whom it commended itself were cast in a different mould and drew their inspiration from other traditions. In their view the system which the Church had been the main agency in organising, had fallen quite as much from its own irremediable weakness as from the direct onslaughts of assailants within and without. The barbarians had rushed in, it was true, in 1793; but this time it was the Church and feudalism which were in the position of the old empire on whose ruins they had built. What had once restored order and belief to the West, was now in its own turn overtaken by decay and dissolution. To look to them to unite these new barbarians in a stable and vigorous civilisation, because they had organised Europe of old, was as infatuated as it would have been to expect the later emperors to equal the exploits of the Republic and their greatest predecessors in the purple. To despise philosophers and men of science was only to play over again in a new dress the very part which Julian had enacted in the face of nascent Christianity. The eighteenth century, instead of being that home of malaria which the Catholic and Royalist party represented, was in truth the seed-ground of a new and better future. Its ideas were to furnish the material and the implements by which should be repaired the terrible breaches and chasms in European order that had been made alike by despots and Jacobins, by priests and atheists, by aristocrats and sans-culottes. Amidst all the demolition upon which its leading minds had been so zealously bent, they had been animated by the warmest love of social justice, of human freedom, of equal rights, and by the most fervent and sincere longing to make a nobler happiness more universally attainable by all the children of men. It was to these great principles that we ought eagerly to turn, to liberty, to equality, to brotherhood, if we wished to achieve before the new invaders a work of civilisation and social reconstruction, such as Catholicism and feudalism had achieved for the multitudinous invaders of old.

Such was the difference which divided opinion when men took heart to survey the appalling scene of moral desolation that the cataclysm of '93 had left behind. We may admire the courage of either school. For if the conscience of the Liberals was oppressed by the sanguinary tragedy in which freedom and brotherhood and justice had been consummated, the Catholic and the Royalist were just as sorely burdened with the weight of kingly basenesses and priestly hypocrisies. If the one had some difficulty in interpreting Jacobinism and the Terror, the other was still more severely pressed to interpret the fact and origin and meaning of the Revolution; if the Liberal had Marat and Hébert, the Royalist had Lewis xv., and the Catholic had Dubois and De Rohan. Each school could intrepidly hurl back the taunts of its enemy, and neither of them did full justice to the strong side of the other. Yet we who are, in England at all events, removed a little aside from the centre of this great battle, may perceive that at that time both of the contending hosts fought under honourable banners, and could inscribe upon their shields a rational and intelligible device. Indeed, unless the modern Liberal admits the strength inherent in the cause of his enemies, it is impossible for him to explain to himself the duration and obstinacy of the conflict, the slow advance and occasional repulse of the host in which he has enlisted, and the tardy progress that Liberalism has made in that stupendous reconstruction which the Revolution has forced the modern political thinker to meditate upon, and the modern statesman to further and control.

De Maistre, from those general ideas as to the method of the government of the world, of which we have already seen something, had formed what he conceived to be a perfectly satisfactory way of accounting for the eighteenth century and its terrific climax. The will of man is left free; he acts contrary to the will of God; and then God exacts the shedding of blood as the penalty. So much for the past. The only hope of the future lay in an immediate return to the system which God himself had established, and in the restoration of that spiritual power which had presided over the reconstruction of Europe in darker and more chaotic times than even these. Though, perhaps, he nowhere expresses himself on this point in a distinct formula, De Maistre was firmly impressed with the idea of historic unity and continuity. He looked upon the history of the West in its integrity, and was entirely free from anything like that disastrous kind of misconception which makes the English Protestant treat the long period between St. Paul and Martin Luther as a howling waste, or which makes some Americans omit from all account the still longer period of human effort from the crucifixion of Christ to the Declaration of Independence. The rise of the vast structure of Western civilisation during and after the dissolution of the Empire, presented itself to his mind as a single and uniform process, though marked in portions by temporary, casual, parenthetical interruptions, due to depraved will and disordered pride. All the dangers to which this civilisation had been exposed in its infancy and growth were before his eyes. First, there were the heresies with which the subtle and debased ingenuity of the Greeks had stained and distorted the great but simple mysteries of the faith. Then came the hordes of invaders from the North, sweeping with irresistible force over regions that the weakness or cowardice of the wearers of the purple left defenceless before them. Before the northern tribes had settled in their possessions, and had full time to assimilate the faith and the institutions which they had found there, the growing organisation was menaced by a more deadly peril in the incessant and steady advance of the bloody and fanatical tribes from the East. And in this way De Maistre's mind continued the picture down to the latest days of all, when there had arisen men who, denying God and mocking at Christ, were bent on the destruction of the very foundations of society, and had nothing better to offer the human race than a miserable return to a state of nature.

As he thus reproduced this long drama, one benign and central figure was ever present, changeless in the midst of ceaseless change; laboriously building up with preterhuman patience and preterhuman sagacity, when other powers, one after another in evil succession, were madly raging to destroy and to pull down; thinking only of the great interests of order and civilisation, of which it had been constituted the eternal protector, and showing its divine origin and inspiration alike by its unfailing wisdom and its unfailing benevolence. It is the Sovereign Pontiff who thus stands forth throughout the history of Europe, as the great Demiurgus of universal civilisation. If the Pope had filled only such a position as the Patriarch held at Constantinople, or if there had been no Pope, and Christianity had depended exclusively on the East for its propagation, with no great spiritual organ in the West, what would have become of Western development? It was the energy and resolution of the Pontiffs which resisted the heresies of the East, and preserved to the Christian religion that plainness and intelligibility, without which it would never have made a way to the rude understanding and simple hearts of the barbarians from the North. It was their wise patriotism which protected Italy against Greek oppression, and by acting the part of mayors of the palace to the decrepit Eastern emperors, it was they who contrived to preserve the independence and maintain the fabric of society until the appearance of the Carlovingians, in whom, with the rapid instinct of true statesmen, they at once recognised the founders of a new empire of the West. If the Popes, again, had possessed over the Eastern empire the same authority that they had over the Western, they would have repulsed not only the Saracens, but the Turks too, and none of the evils which these nations have inflicted on us would ever have taken place.[10] Even as it was, when the Saracens threatened the West, the

Popes were the chief agents in organising resistance, and giving spirit and animation to the defenders of Europe. Their alert vision saw that to crush for ever that formidable enemy, it was not enough to defend ourselves against his assaults; we must attack him at home. The Crusades, vulgarly treated as the wars of a blind and superstitious piety, were in truth wars of high policy. From the Council of Clermont down to the famous day of Lepanto, the hand and spirit of the Pontiff were to be traced in every part of that tremendous struggle which prevented Europe from being handed over to the tyranny, ignorance, and barbarism that have always been the inevitable fruits of Mahometan conquest, and had already stamped out civilisation in Asia Minor and Palestine and Greece, once the very garden of the universe.

This admirable and politic heroism of the Popes in the face of foes pressing from without, De Maistre found more than equalled by their wisdom, courage, and activity in organising and developing the elements of a civilised system within. The maxim of old societies had been that which Lucan puts into the mouth of Cæsar—*humanum paucis vivit genus*. A vast population of slaves had been one of the inevitable social conditions of the period: the Popes never rested from their endeavours to banish servitude from among Christian nations. Women in old societies had filled a mean and degraded place: it was reserved for the new spiritual power to rescue the race from that vicious circle in which men had debased the nature of women, and women had given back all the weakness and perversity they had received from men, and to perceive that 'the most effectual way of perfecting the man is to ennoble and exalt the woman.' The organisation of the priesthood, again, was a masterpiece of practical wisdom. Such an order, removed from the fierce or selfish interests of ordinary life by the holy regulation of celibacy, and by the austere discipline of the Church, was indispensable in the midst of such a society as that which it was the function of the Church to guide. Who but the members of an order thus set apart, acting in strict subordination to the central power, and so presenting a front of unbroken spiritual unity, could have held their way among tumultuous tribes, half-barbarous nobles, and proud and unruly kings, protesting against wrong, passionately inculcating new and higher ideas of right, denouncing the darkness of the false gods, calling on all men to worship the cross and adore the mysteries of the true God? Compare now the impotency of the Protestant missionary, squatting in gross comfort with wife and babes among the savages he has come to convert, preaching a disputatious doctrine, wrangling openly with the rival sent by some other sect—compare this impotency with the success that follows the devoted sons of the Church, impressing their proselytes with the mysterious virtue of their continence, the self-denial of their lives, the unity of their dogma and their rites; and then recognise the wisdom of these great churchmen who created a priesthood after this manner in the days when every priest was as the missionary is now. Finally, it was the occupants of the holy chair who prepared, softened, one might almost say sweetened, the occupants of thrones; it was to them that Providence had confided the education of the sovereigns of Europe. The Popes brought up the youth of the European monarchy; they made it precisely in the same way in which Fénelon made the Duke of Burgundy. In each case the task consisted in eradicating from a fine character an element of ferocity that would have ruined all. 'Everything that constrains a man strengthens him. He cannot obey without perfecting himself; and by the mere fact of overcoming himself he is better. Any man will vanquish the most violent passion at thirty, because at five or six you have taught him of his own will to give up a plaything or a sweetmeat. That came to pass to the monarchy, which happens to an individual who has been well brought up. The continued efforts of the Church, directed by the Sovereign Pontiff, did what had never been seen before, and what will never be seen again where that authority is not recognised. Insensibly, without threats or laws or battles, without violence and without resistance, the great European charter was proclaimed, not on paper nor by the voice of public criers; but in all European hearts, then all Catholic Kings surrender the power of judging by themselves, and nations in return declare kings infallible and inviolable. Such is the fundamental law of the European monarchy, and it is the work of the Popes.'[11]

All this, however, is only the external development of De Maistre's central idea, the historical corroboration of a truth to which he conducts us in the first instance by general considerations. Assuming, what it is less and less characteristic of the present century at any rate to deny, that Christianity was the only actual force by which the regeneration of Europe could be effected after the decline of the Roman civilisation, he insists that, as he again and again expresses it, 'without the Pope there is no veritable Christianity.' What he meant by this condensed form needs a little explanation, as is always the case with such simple statements of the products of long and complex reasoning. In saying that without the Pope there is no true Christianity, what he considered himself as having established was, that unless there be some supreme and independent possessor of authority to settle doctrine, to regulate discipline, to give authentic counsel, to apply accepted principles to disputed cases, then there can be no such thing as a religious system which shall have power to bind the members of a vast and not homogeneous body in the salutary bonds of a common civilisation, nor to guide and inform an universal conscience. In each individual state everybody admits the absolute necessity of having some sovereign power which shall make, declare, and administer the laws, and from whose action in any one of these aspects there shall be no appeal; a power that shall be strong enough to protect the rights and enforce the duties which it has authoritatively proclaimed and enjoined. In free England, as in despotic Turkey, the privileges and obligations which the law tolerates or imposes, and all the benefits which their existence confers on the community, are the creatures and conditions of a supreme authority from which there is no appeal, whether the instrument by which this authority makes its will known be an act of parliament or a ukase. This conception of temporal sovereignty, especially familiarised to our generation by the teaching of Austin, was carried by De Maistre into discussions upon the limits of the Papal power with great ingenuity and force, and, if we accept the premisses, with great success.

It should be said here, that throughout his book on the Pope, De Maistre talks of Christianity exclusively as a statesman or a publicist would talk about it; not theologically nor spiritually, but politically and socially. The question with which he concerns himself is the utilisation of Christianity as a force to shape and organise a system of civilised societies; a study of the conditions under which this utilisation had taken place in the earlier centuries of the era; and a deduction from them of the conditions under which we might ensure a repetition of the process in changed modern circumstance. In the eighteenth century men were accustomed to ask of Christianity, as Protestants always ask of so much of Catholicism as they have dropped, whether or no it is true. But after the Revolution the question changed, and became an inquiry whether and how Christianity could contribute to the reconstruction of society. People asked less how true it was, than how strong it was; less how many unquestioned dogmas, than how much social weight it had or could develop; less as to the precise amount and form of belief that would save a soul, than as to the way in which it might be expected to assist the European community.

It was the strength of this temper in him which led to his extraordinary detestation and contempt for the Greeks. Their turn for pure speculation excited all his anger. In a curious chapter, he exhausts invective in denouncing them.[12] The sarcasm of Sallust delights him, that the actions of Greece were very fine, *verum aliquanto minores quam fama feruntur*. Their military glory was only a flash of about a hundred and fourteen years from Marathon; compare this with the prolonged splendour of Rome, France, and England. In philosophy they displayed decent talent, but even here their true merit is to have brought the wisdom of Asia into Europe, for they invented nothing. Greece was the home of syllogism and of unreason. 'Read Plato: at every page you will draw a striking distinction. As often as he is Greek, he wearies you. He is only great, sublime, penetrating, when he is a theologian; in other words, when he is announcing positive and everlasting dogmas, free from all quibble, and which are so clearly marked with the eastern cast, that not to perceive it one must never have had a glimpse of Asia.... There was in him a sophist and a theologian, or, if you choose, a Greek and a Chaldean.' The Athenians could never pardon one of their great leaders, all of whom fell victims in one shape or another to a temper frivolous as that of a child, ferocious as that of men,—'*espèce de moutons enragés, toujours menés par la nature, et toujours par nature dévorant leurs bergers.*' As for their oratory, 'the tribune of Athens would have been the disgrace of mankind if Phocion and men like him, by occasionally ascending it before drinking the hemlock or setting out for their place of exile, had not in some sort balanced such a mass of loquacity, extravagance, and cruelty.'[13]

It is very important to remember this constant solicitude for ideas that should work well, in connection with that book of De Maistre's which has had most influence in Europe, by supplying a base for the theories of ultramontanism. Unless we perceive very clearly that throughout his ardent speculations on the Papal power his mind was bent upon enforcing the practical solution of a pressing social problem, we easily misunderstand him and underrate what he had to say. A charge has been forcibly urged against him by an eminent English critic, for example, that he has confounded supremacy with infallibility, than which, as the writer truly says, no two ideas can be more perfectly distinct, one being superiority of force, and the other incapacity of error.[14] De Maistre made logical blunders in abundance quite as bad as this, but he was too acute, I think, deliberately to erect so elaborate a structure upon a confusion so very obvious, and that must have stared him in the face from the first page of his work to the last. If we look upon his book as a mere general defence of the Papacy, designed to investigate and fortify all its pretensions one by one, we should have great right to complain against having two claims so essentially divergent, treated as though they were the same thing, or could be held in their places by the same supports. But let us regard the treatise on the Pope not as meant to convince free-thinkers or Protestants that divine grace inspires every decree of the Holy Father, though that would have been the right view of it if it had been written fifty years earlier. It was composed within the first twenty years of the present century, when the universe, to men of De Maistre's stamp, seemed once more without form and void. His object, as he tells us more than once, was to find a way of restoring a religion and a morality in Europe; of giving to truth the forces demanded for the conquests that she was meditating; of strengthening the thrones of sovereigns, and of gently calming that general fermentation of spirit which threatened mightier evils than any that had yet overwhelmed society. From this point of view we shall see that the distinction between supremacy and infallibility was not worth recognising.

Practically, he says, 'infallibility is only a consequence of supremacy, or rather it is absolutely the same thing under two different names.... In effect it is the same thing, *in practice*, not to be subject to error, and not to be liable to be accused of it. Thus, even if we should agree that no divine promise was made to the Pope, he would not be less infallible or deemed so, as the final tribunal; for every judgment from which you cannot appeal is and must be (*est et doit être*) held for just in every human association, under any imaginable form of government; and every true statesman will understand me perfectly, when I say that the point is to ascertain not only if the Sovereign Pontiff is, but if he must be, infallible.'[15] In another place he says distinctly enough that the infallibility of the Church has two aspects; in one of them it is the object of divine promise, in the other it is a human implication, and that in the latter aspect infallibility is supposed in the Church, just 'as we are absolutely bound to suppose it, even in temporal sovereignties (where it does not really exist), under pain of seeing society dissolved.' The Church only demands what other sovereignties demand, though she has the immense superiority over them of having her claim backed by direct promise from heaven.[16] Take away the dogma, if you will, he says, and only consider the thing politically, which is exactly what he really does all through the book. The pope, from this point of view, asks for no other infallibility than that which is attributed to all sovereigns.[17] Without either vindicating or surrendering the supernatural side of the Papal claims, he only insists upon the political, social, or human side of it, as an inseparable quality of an admitted supremacy.[18] In short, from beginning to end of this speculation, from which the best kind of ultramontanism has drawn its defence, he evinces a deprecatory anxiety—a very rare temper with De Maistre—not to fight on the issue of the dogma of infallibility over which Protestants and unbelievers have won an infinite number of cheap victories; that he leaves as a theme more fitted for the disputations of theologians. My position, he seems to keep saying, is that if the Pope is spiritually supreme, then he is virtually and practically *as if he were* infallible, just in the same sense in which the English Parliament and monarch, and the Russian Czar, are as if they were infallible. But let us not argue so much about this, which is only secondary. The main question is whether without the Pope there can be a true Christianity, 'that is to say, a Christianity, active, powerful, converting, regenerating, conquering, perfecting.'

De Maistre was probably conducted to his theory by an analogy, which he tacitly leaned upon more strongly than it could well bear, between temporal organisation and spiritual organisation. In inchoate communities, the momentary self-interest and the promptly stirred passions of men would rend the growing society in pieces, unless they were restrained by the strong hand of law in some shape or other, written or unwritten, and administered by an authority, either physically too strong to be resisted, or else set up by the common consent seeking to further the general convenience. To divide this authority, so that none should know where to look for a sovereign decree, nor be able to ascertain the commands of sovereign law; to embody it in the persons of many discordant expounders, each assuming oracular weight and equal sanction; to leave individuals to administer and interpret it for themselves, and to decide among themselves its application to their own cases; what would this be but a deliberate preparation for anarchy and dissolution? For it is one of the clear conditions of the efficacy of the social union, that every member of it should be able to know for certain the terms on which he belongs to it, the compliances which it will insist upon in him, and the compliances which it will in turn permit him to insist upon in others, and therefore it is indispensable that there should be some definite and admitted centre where this very essential knowledge should be accessible.

Some such reflections as these must have been at the bottom of De Maistre's great apology for the Papal supremacy, or at any rate they may serve to bring before our minds with greater clearness the kind of foundations on which his scheme rested. For law substitute Christianity, for social union spiritual union, for legal obligations the obligations of the faith. Instead of individuals bound together by allegiance to common political institutions, conceive communities united in the bonds of religious brotherhood into a sort of universal republic, under the moderate supremacy of a supreme spiritual power. As a matter of fact, it was the intervention of this spiritual power which restrained the anarchy, internal and external, of the ferocious and imperfectly organised sovereignties that figure in the early history of modern Europe. And as a matter of theory, what could be more rational and defensible than such an intervention made systematic, with its rightfulness and disinterestedness universally recognised? Grant Christianity as the spiritual basis of the life and action of modern communities; supporting both the organised structure of each of them, and the interdependent system composed of them all; accepted by the individual members of each, and by the integral bodies forming the whole. But who shall declare what the Christian doctrine is, and how its maxims bear upon special cases, and what oracles they announce in particular sets of circumstances? Amid the turbulence of popular passion, in face of the crushing despotism of an insensate tyrant, between the furious hatred of jealous nations or the violent ambition of rival sovereigns, what likelihood would there be of either party to the contention yielding tranquilly and promptly to any presentation of Christian teaching made by the other, or by some suspected neutral as a decisive authority between them? Obviously there must be some supreme and indisputable interpreter, before whose final decree the tyrant should quail, the flood of popular lawlessness flow back within its accustomed banks, and contending sovereigns or jealous nations fraternally embrace. Again, in those questions of faith and discipline, which the ill-exercised ingenuity of men is for ever raising and pressing upon the attention of Christendom, it is just as obvious that there must be some tribunal to pronounce an authoritative judgment. Otherwise, each nation is torn into sects; and amid the throng of sects where is unity? 'To maintain that a crowd of independent churches form a church, one and universal, is to maintain in other terms that all the political governments of Europe only form a single government, one and universal.' There could no more be a kingdom of France without a king, nor an empire of Russia without an emperor, than there could be one universal church without an acknowledged head. That this head must be the successor of St. Peter, is declared alike by the voice of tradition, the explicit testimony of the early writers, the repeated utterances of later theologians of all schools, and that general sentiment which presses itself upon every conscientious reader of religious history.

The argument that the voice of the Church is to be sought in general councils is absurd. To maintain that a council has any other function than to assure and certify the Pope, when he chooses to strengthen his judgment or to satisfy his doubts, is to destroy visible unity. Suppose there to be an equal division of votes, as happened in the famous case of Fénelon, and might as well happen in a general council, the doubt would after all be solved by the final vote of the Pope. And 'what is doubtful for twenty selected men is doubtful for the whole human race. Those who suppose that by multiplying the deliberating voices doubt is lessened, must have very little knowledge of men, and can never have sat in a deliberative body.' Again, supposing there to present itself one of those questions of divine metaphysics that it is absolutely necessary to refer to the decision of the supreme tribunal. Then our interest is not that it should be decided in such or such a manner, but that it should be decided without delay and without appeal. Besides, the world is now grown too vast for general councils, which seem to be made only for the youth of Christianity. In fine, why pursue futile or mischievous discussions as to whether the Pope is above the Council or the Council above the Pope? In ordinary questions in which a king is conscious of sufficient light, he decides them himself, while the others in which he is not conscious of this light, he transfers to the States-General presided over by himself, but he is equally sovereign in either case. So with the Pope and the Council. Let us be content to know, in the words of Thomassin, [19] that 'the Pope in the midst of his Council is above himself, and that the Council decapitated of its chief is below him.'

The point so constantly dwelt upon by Bossuet, the obligation of the canons upon the Pope, was of very little worth in De Maistre's judgment, and he almost speaks with disrespect of the great Catholic defender for being so prolix and pertinacious in elaborating it. Here again he finds in Thomassin the most concise statement of what he held to be the true view, just as he does in the controversy as to the relative superiority of the Pope or the Council. 'There is only an apparent contradiction,' says Thomassin, 'between saying that the Pope is above the canons, and that he is bound by them; that he is master of the canons, or that he is not. Those who place him above the canons or make him their master, only pretend that he *has a dispensing power over them;* while those who deny that he is above the canons or is their master, mean no more than that *he can only exercise a dispensing power for the convenience and in the necessities of the Church.'* This is an excellent illustration of the thoroughly political temper in which De Maistre treats the whole subject. He looks at the power of the Pope over the canons much as a modern English statesman looks at the question of the coronation oath, and the extent to which it binds the monarch to the maintenance of the laws existing at the time of its imposition. In the same spirit he banishes from all account the crowd of nonsensical objections to Papal supremacy, drawn from imaginary possibilities. Suppose a Pope, for example, were to abolish all the canons at a single stroke; suppose him to become an unbeliever; suppose him to go mad; and so forth. 'Why,' De Maistre says, 'there is not in the whole world a single power in a condition to bear all possible and arbitrary hypotheses of this sort; and if you judge them by what they can do, without speaking of what they have done, they will have to be abolished every one.'[20] This, it may be worth noticing, is one of the many passages in De Maistre's writings which, both in the solidity of their argument and the direct force of their expression, recall his great predecessor in the anti-revolutionary cause, the ever-illustrious Burke.

The vigour with which De Maistre sums up all these pleas for supremacy is very remarkable; and to the crowd of enemies and indifferents, and especially to the statesmen who are among them, he appeals with admirable energy. 'What do you want, then? Do you mean that the nations should live without any religion, and do you not begin to perceive that a religion there must be? And does not Christianity, not only by its intrinsic worth but because it is in possession, strike you as preferable to every other? Have you been better contented with other attempts in this way? Peradventure the twelve apostles might please you better than the Theophilanthropists and Martinists? Does the Sermon on the Mount seem to you a passable code of morals? And if the entire people were to regulate their conduct on this model, should you be content? I fancy that I hear you reply affirmatively. Well, since the only object now is to maintain this religion for which you thus declare your preference, how could you have, I do not say the stupidity, but the cruelty, to turn it into a democracy, and to place this precious deposit in the hands of the rabble?

'You attach too much importance to the dogmatic part of this religion. By what strange contradiction would you desire to agitate the universe for some academic quibble, for miserable wranglings about mere words (these are your own terms)? Is it so then that men are led? Will you call the Bishop of Quebec and the Bishop of Luçon to interpret a line of the Catechism? That believers should quarrel about infallibility is what I know, for I see it; but that statesmen should quarrel in the same way about this great privilege, is what I shall never be able to conceive.... That all the bishops in the world should be convoked to determine a divine truth necessary to salvation—nothing more natural, if such a method is indispensable; for no effort, no trouble, ought to be spared for so exalted an aim. But if the only point is the establishment of one opinion in the place of another, then the travelling expenses of even one single Infallible are sheer waste. If you want to spare the two most valuable things on earth, time and money, make all haste to write to Rome, in order to procure thence a lawful decision which shall declare the unlawful doubt. Nothing more is needed; policy asks no more.'[21]

Definitely, then, the influence of the Popes restored to their ancient supremacy would be exercised in the renewal and consolidation of social order resting on the Christian faith, somewhat after this manner. The anarchic dogma of the sovereignty of peoples, having failed to do anything beyond showing that the greatest evils resulting from obedience do not equal the thousandth part of those which result from rebellion, would be superseded by the practice of appeals to the authority of the Holy See. Do not suppose that the Revolution is at an end, or that the column is replaced because it is raised up from the ground. A man must be blind not to see that all the sovereignties in Europe are growing weak; on all sides confidence and affection are deserting them; sects and the spirit of individualism are multiplying themselves in an appalling manner. There are only two alternatives: you must either purify the will of men, or else you must enchain it; the monarch who will not do the first, must enslave his subjects or perish; servitude or spiritual unity is the only choice open to nations. On the one hand is the gross and unrestrained tyranny of what in modern phrase is styled Imperialism, and on the other a wise and benevolent modification of temporal sovereignty in the interests of all by an established and accepted spiritual power. No middle path lies before the people of Europe. Temporal absolutism we must have. The only question is whether or no it shall be modified by the wise, disinterested, and moderating counsels of the Church, as given by her consecratèd chief.

There can be very little doubt that the effective way in which De Maistre propounded and vindicated this theory made a deep impression on the mind of Comte. Very early in his career this eminent man had declared: 'De Maistre has for me the peculiar property of helping me to estimate the philosophic capacity of people, by the repute in which they hold him.' Among his other reasons at that time for thinking well of M. Guizot was that, notwithstanding his transcendent Protestantism, he complied with the test of appreciating De Maistre.[22] Comte's rapidly assimilative intelligence perceived that here at last there was a definite, consistent, and intelligible scheme for the reorganisation of European society, with him the great end of philosophic endeavour. Its principle of the division of the spiritual and temporal powers, and of the relation that ought to subsist between the two, was the base of Comte's own scheme.

In general form the plans of social reconstruction are identical; in substance, it need scarcely be said, the differences are fundamental. The temporal power, according to Comte's design, is to reside with industrial chiefs, and the spiritual power to rest upon a doctrine scientifically established. De Maistre, on the other hand, believed that the old authority of kings and Christian pontiffs was divine, and any attempt to supersede it in either case would have seemed to him as desperate as it seemed impious. In his strange speculation on *Le Principe Générateur des Constitutions Politiques*, he contends that all laws in the true sense of the word (which by the way happens to be decidedly an arbitrary and exclusive sense) are of supernatural origin, and that the only persons whom we have any right to call legislators, are those half-divine men who appear mysteriously in the early history of nations, and counterparts to whom we never meet in later days. Elsewhere he maintains to the same effect, that royal families in the true sense of the word 'are growths of nature, and differ from others, as a tree differs from a shrub.'

People suppose a family to be royal because it reigns; on the contrary, it reigns because it is royal, because it has more life, *plus d'esprit royal —* surely as mysterious and occult a force as the *virtus dormitiva* of opium. The common life of man is about thirty years; the average duration of the reigns of European sovereigns, being Christian, is at the very lowest calculation twenty. How is it possible that 'lives should be only thirty years, and reigns from twenty-two to twenty-five, if princes had not more common life than other men?' Mark again, the influence of religion in the duration of sovereignties. All the Christian reigns are longer than all the non-Christian reigns, ancient and modern, and Catholic reigns have been longer than Protestant reigns. The reigns in England, which averaged more than twenty-three years before the Reformation, have only been seventeen years since that, and those of Sweden, which were twenty-two, have fallen to the same figure of seventeen. Denmark, however, for some unknown cause does not appear to have undergone this law of abbreviation; so, says De Maistre with rather unwonted restraint, let us abstain from generalising. As a matter of fact, however, the generalisation was complete in his own mind, and there was nothing inconsistent with his view of the government of the universe in the fact that a Catholic prince should live longer than a Protestant; indeed such a fact was the natural condition of his view being true. Many differences among the people who hold to the theological interpretation of the circumstances of life arise from the different degrees of activity which they variously attribute to the intervention of God, from those who explain the fall of a sparrow to the ground by a special and direct energy of the divine will, up to those at the opposite end of the scale, who think that direct participation ended when the universe was once fairly launched. De Maistre was of those who see the divine hand on every side and at all times. If, then, Protestantism was a pernicious rebellion against the faith which God had provided for the comfort and salvation of men, why should not God be likely to visit princes, as offenders with the least excuse for their backslidings, with the curse of shortness of days?

In a trenchant passage De Maistre has expounded the Protestant confession of faith, and shown what astounding gaps it leaves as an interpretation of the dealings of God with man. 'By virtue of a terrible anathema,' he supposes the Protestant to say, 'inexplicable no doubt, but much less inexplicable than incontestable, the human race lost all its rights. Plunged in mortal darkness, it was ignorant of all, since it was ignorant of God; and, being ignorant of him, it could not pray to him, so that it was spiritually dead without being able to ask for life. Arrived by rapid degradation at the last stage of debasement, it outraged nature by its manners, its laws, even by its religions. It consecrated all vices, it wallowed in filth, and its depravation was such that the history of those times forms a dangerous picture, which it is not good for all men so much as to look upon. God, however, *having dissembled for forty centuries*, bethought him of his creation. At the appointed moment announced from all time, he did not despise a virgin's womb; he clothed himself in our unhappy nature, and appeared on the earth; we saw him, we touched him, he spoke to us; he lived, he taught, he suffered, he died for us. He arose from his tomb according to his promise; he appeared again among us, solemnly to assure to his Church a succour that would last as long as the world.

'But, alas, this effort of almighty benevolence was a long way from securing all the success that had been foretold. For lack of knowledge, or of strength, or by distraction maybe, God missed his aim, and could not keep his word. Less sage than a chemist who should undertake to shut up ether in canvas or paper, he only confided to men the truth that he had brought upon the earth; it escaped, then, as one might have foreseen, by all human pores; soon, this holy religion revealed to man by the Man-God, became no more than an infamous idolatry, which would remain to this very moment if Christianity after sixteen centuries had not been suddenly brought back to its original purity by a couple of sorry creatures.'[23]

Perhaps it would be easier than he supposed to present his own system in an equally irrational aspect. If you measure the proceedings of omnipotence by the uses to which a wise and benevolent man would put such superhuman power, if we can imagine a man of this kind endowed with it, De Maistre's theory of the extent to which a supreme being interferes in human things, is after all only a degree less ridiculous and illogical, less inadequate and abundantly assailable, than that Protestantism which he so heartily despised. Would it be difficult, after borrowing the account, which we have just read, of the tremendous efforts made by a benign creator to shed moral and spiritual light upon the world, to perplex the Catholic as bitterly as the Protestant, by confronting him both with the comparatively scanty results of those efforts, and with the too visible tendencies of all the foremost agencies in modern civilisation to leave them out of account as forces practically spent?

De Maistre has been surpassed by no thinker that we know of as a defender of the old order. If anybody could rationalise the idea of supernatural intervention in human affairs, the idea of a Papal supremacy, the idea of a spiritual unity, De Maistre's acuteness and intellectual vigour, and, above all, his keen sense of the urgent social need of such a thing being done, would assuredly have enabled him to do it. In 1817, when he wrote the work in which this task is attempted, the hopelessness of such an achievement was less obvious than it is now. The Bourbons had been restored. The Revolution lay in a deep slumber that many persons excusably took for the quiescence of extinction. Legitimacy and the spiritual system that was its ally in the face of the Revolution, though mostly its rival or foe when they were left alone together, seemed to be restored to the fulness of their power. Fifty years have elapsed since then, and each year has seen a progressive decay in the principles which then were triumphant. It was not, therefore, without reason that De Maistre warned people against believing *'que la colonne est replacée, parcequ'elle est relevée.'* The solution which he so elaborately recommended to Europe has shown itself desperate and impossible. Catholicism may long remain a vital creed to millions of men, a deep source of spiritual consolation and refreshment, and a bright lamp in perplexities of conduct and morals; but resting on dogmas which cannot by any amount of compromise be incorporated with the daily increasing mass of knowledge, assuming as the condition of its existence forms of the theological hypothesis which all the preponderating influences of contemporary thought concur directly or indirectly in discrediting, upheld by an organisation which its history for the last five centuries has exposed to the distrust and hatred of men as the sworn enemy of mental freedom and growth, the pretensions of Catholicism to renovate society are among the most pitiable and impotent that ever devout, high-minded, and benevolent persons deluded themselves into maintaining or accepting. Over the modern invader it is as powerless as paganism was over the invaders of old. The barbarians of industrialism, grasping chiefs and mutinous men, give no ear to priest or pontiff, who speak only dead words, who confront modern issues with blind eyes, and who stretch out a palsied hand to help. Christianity, according to a well-known saying, has been tried and failed; the religion of Christ remains to be tried. One would prefer to qualify the first clause, by admitting how much Christianity has done for Europe even with its old organisation, and to restrict the charge of failure within the limits of the modern time. To-day its failure is too patent. Whether in changed forms and with new supplements the teaching of its founder is destined to be the chief inspirer of that social and human sentiment which seems to be the only spiritual bond capable of uniting men together again in a common and effective faith, is a question which it is unnecessary to discuss here. *'They talk about the first centuries of Christianity,'* said De Maistre, *'I would not be sure that they are over yet.'* Perhaps not; only if the first centuries are not yet over, it is certain that the Christianity of the future will have to be so different from the Christianity of the past, as to demand or deserve another name.

Even if Christianity, itself renewed, could successfully encounter the achievement of renewing society, De Maistre's ideal of a spiritual power controlling the temporal power, and conciliating peoples with their rulers by persuasion and a coercion only moral, appears to have little chance of being realised. The separation of the two powers is sealed, with a completeness that is increasingly visible. The principles on which the process of the emancipation of politics is being so rapidly carried on, demonstrate that the most marked tendencies of modern civilisation are strongly hostile to a renewal in any imaginable shape, or at any future time, of a connection whether of virtual subordination or nominal equality, which has laid such enormous burdens on the consciences and understandings of men. If the Church has the uppermost hand, except in primitive times, it destroys freedom; if the State is supreme, it destroys spirituality. The free Church in the free State is an idea that every day more fully recommends itself to the public opinion of Europe, and the sovereignty of the Pope, like that of all other spiritual potentates, can only be exercised over those who choose of their own accord to submit to it; a sovereignty of a kind which De Maistre thought not much above anarchy.

To conclude, De Maistre's mind was of the highest type of those who fill the air with the arbitrary assumptions of theology, and the abstractions of the metaphysical stage of thought. At every point you meet the peremptorily declared volition of a divine being, or the ontological property of a natural object. The French Revolution is explained by the will of God; and the kings reign because they have the *esprit royal*. Every truth is absolute, not relative; every explanation is universal, not historic. These differences in method and point of view amply explain his arrival at conclusions that seem so monstrous to men who look upon all knowledge as relative, and insist that the only possible road to true opinion lies away from volitions and abstractions in the positive generalisations of experience. There can be no more satisfactory proof of the rapidity with which we are leaving these ancient methods, and the social results which they produced, than the willingness with which every rightly instructed mind now admits how indispensable were the first, and how beneficial the second. Those can best appreciate De Maistre and his school, what excellence lay in their aspirations, what wisdom in their system, who know most clearly why their aspirations were hopeless, and what makes their system an anachronism.

FOOTNOTES:

[1] See Damiron's *La Philosophie en France au XIXième Siècle.* Introduction to Vol. I. (Fifth edition.)

[2] The facts of De Maistre's life I have drawn from a very meagre biography by his son, Count Rodolphe de Maistre, supplemented by two volumes of *Lettres et Opuscules* (Fourth edition. Paris: Vaton. 1865), and a volume of his *Diplomatic Correspondence*, edited by M. Albert Blanc.

[3] *Soirées de Saint Pétersbourg* (8th ed. 1862), vol. i. pp. 238-243.

[4] *Soirées de Saint Pétersbourg, 6ième entretien*, i. 397-442.

[5] *Ib.* (8th ed. 1862) vol. i. p. 403.

[6] *Soirées*, i. 76

[7] De Maistre found a curiously characteristic kind of support for this view in the fact that evils are called *fléaux:* flails are things to beat with: so evils must be things with which men are beaten; and as we should not be beaten if we did not deserve it, *argal*, suffering is a merited punishment. Apart from that common infirmity which leads people after they have discovered an analogy between two things, to argue from the properties of the one to those of the other, as if, instead of being analogous, they were identical, De Maistre was particularly fond of inferring moral truths from etymologies. He has an argument for the deterioration of man, drawn from the fact that the Romans expressed in the same word, *supplicium*, the two ideas of prayer and punishment (*Soirées, 2ième entretien*, i. p. 108). His profundity as an etymologist may be gathered from his analysis of *cadaver: ca*-ro, *da*-ta, *ver*-mibus. There are many others of the same quality.

[8] *Gibbon*, c. xlvi. vol. v. 385.

[9] See the *Examen de la Philosophie de Bacon*, vol. ii. 58 *et seq.*

[10] De Maistre forgot or underestimated the services of Leo the Isaurian whose repulse of the Caliph's forces at Constantinople (a.d. 717) was perhaps as important for Europe as the more renowned victory of Charles Martel. But then Leo was an Iconoclast and heretic. Cf. Finlay's *Byzantine Empire*, pp. 22, 23.

[11] *Du Pape*, bk. iii. c. iv. p. 298 (ed. 1866).

[12] *Du Pape*, bk. iv. c. vii.

[13] A remark of Mr. Finlay's is worth quoting here. 'The Greeks,' he says, 'had at times only a secondary share in the ecclesiastical controversies in the Eastern Church, though the circumstance of these controversies having been carried on in the Greek language has made the natives of Western Europe attribute them to a philosophic, speculative, and polemic spirit, inherent in the Hellenic mind. A very slight examination of history is sufficient to prove that several of the heresies which disturbed the Eastern Church had their origin in the more profound religious ideas of the oriental nations, and that many of the opinions called heretical were in a great measure expressions of the mental nationality of the Syrians, Armenians, Egyptians, and Persians, and had no conception whatever with the Greek mind.'—*Byzantine Empire, from 716 to 1057*, p. 262.

The same writer remarks very truly, that 'the religious or theological portion of Popery, as a section of the Christian Church, is really Greek; and it is only the ecclesiastical, political, and theoretic peculiarities of the fabric which can be considered as the work of the Latin Church.'

[14] Sir J. Fitzjames Stephen in the *Saturday Review*, Sept. 9, 1865, p. 334.

[15] *Du Pape*, bk. i. c. i. p. 17.

[16] *Ib.* bk. i. c. xix. pp. 124, 125.

[17] *Ib.* bk. i. c. xvi. p. 111.

[18] '*Il n'y a point de souveraineté qui pour le bonheur des hommes, et pour le sien surtout, ne soit bornée de quelque manière, mais dans l'intérieur de ces bornes, placées comme il plaît à Dieu, elle est toujours et partout absolue et tenue pour infaillible. Et quand je parle de l'exercice légitime de la souveraineté, je n'entends point ou je ne dis point l'exercice* juste, ce qui produirait une amphibologie dangereuse, à moins que par ce dernier mot on ne veuille dire que tout ce qu'elle opine dans son cercle est* juste ou tenu pour tel, ce qui est la vérité. C'est ainsi qu'un tribunal suprême, tant qu'il ne sort pas de ses attributions, est toujours juste;* car c'est la même chose dans la pratique, d'être infaillible, ou de se tromper sans appel.'—Bk. ii. c. xi. p. 212 (footnote).

[19] Thomassin, the eminent French theologian, flourished from the middle to the end of the seventeenth century. The aim of his writings generally was to reconcile conflicting opinions on discipline or doctrine by exhibiting a true sense in all. In this spirit he wrote on the Pope and the Councils, and on the never-ending question of Grace. Among other

things, he insisted that all languages could be traced to the Hebrew. He wrote a defence of the edict in which Lewis xiv. revoked the Edict of Nantes, contending that it was less harsh than some of the decrees of Theodosius and Justinian, which the holiest fathers of the Church had not scrupled to approve—an argument which would now be thought somewhat too dangerous for common use, as cutting both ways. Gibbon made use of his *Discipline de l'Eglise* in the twentieth chapter, and elsewhere.

[20] *Du Pape*, bk. i. c. xviii. p. 122.

[21] Bk. i. c. xvii. p. 117.

[22] Littré, *Auguste Comte et la Phil. Posit.* p. 152.

[23] *Du Pape*, Conclusion, p. 380.